T0023096

Towards a Green Democratic Revolution

Left Populism and the Power of Affects

Chantal Mouffe

VERSO

London • New York

First published by Verso 2022
© Chantal Mouffe 2022

1 3 5 7 9 10 8 6 4 2

Verso
UK: 6 Meard Street, London W1F 0EG
US: 388 Atlantic Avenue, Brooklyn, NY 11217
versobooks.com

Verso is the imprint of New Left Books

ISBN-13: 978-1-83976-750-0
ISBN-13: 978-1-83976-752-4 (UK EBK)
ISBN-13: 978-1-83976-753-1 (US EBK)

British Library Cataloguing in Publication Data
A catalogue record for this book is available from the British Library

Library of Congress Cataloging-in-Publication Data
A catalog record for this book is available from the Library of Congress

Typeset in Sabon by Hewer Text UK Ltd, Edinburgh
Printed and bound by CPI Group (UK) Ltd, Croydon CR0 4YY

Contents

1
A New Authoritarian
Form of Neoliberalism

In *For a Left Populism*, drawing on the discursive hegemonic approach elaborated in *Hegemony and Socialist Strategy* and on Ernesto Laclau's analysis of populism in *On Populist Reason*, I examined the conjuncture in Western Europe in the years following the 2008 crisis, a conjuncture I designated a 'populist moment'.[1] I showed that it was the expression of varied forms of resistance to the political and economic transformations resulting from thirty years of neoliberal hegemony. These transformations have led to a situation referred to as 'post-democracy' to signal the erosion of the two pillars of the democratic ideal: equality and popular sovereignty.

In the political arena, this evolution is characterized by what I proposed in *On the Political* to call 'post-politics'.[2] By that term, I mean the consensus established between centre-right and centre-left parties on the idea that there was no alternative to neoliberal globalization. Under the pretext of 'modernization' imposed by globalization, social-democratic parties accepted the diktats of financial capitalism and the limits they imposed on state interventions in the field of redistributive policies. Politics became a mere technical issue of managing the established order, a domain reserved for experts. Elections no longer offer any opportunity to decide on real alternatives through the traditional parties of 'government'. The only thing that post-politics allows is a bipartisan alternation of power between the centre-right and centre-left parties. Thus, the power of the people, one of the fundamental pillars of the democratic ideal, has been undermined: popular sovereignty has been declared obsolete, and democracy has been reduced to its liberal component.

These changes at the political level have taken place in the context of a new mode of capitalist regulation in which financial capital occupies a central place. The financialization of the economy has led to a great expansion of the financial sector at the cost of the productive economy. With the effects of the austerity policies imposed after the 2008 crisis, we witnessed an exponential increase in inequality in European countries, particularly in the south. This inequality no longer affects only the working class but also a large part of the middle classes, which have entered into a process of pauperization and precarization. This has contributed to the collapse of that other pillar of the democratic ideal – the defence of equality – which has also been eliminated from the main liberal–democratic discourse. The result of neoliberal hegemony was the establishment, both socio-economically and politically, of a truly oligarchic regime. All those who oppose this post-democratic 'consensus in the centre' are presented as extremists and denounced as populists.

One of the central claims of the book is that it is in the post-democratic context that the 'populist moment' can be understood. To apprehend its dynamics, it is necessary to adopt an anti-essentialist approach according to which the 'people' is envisioned as a political category, not a socio-logical one, or as an empirical referent. The confrontation, people versus establishment, characteristic of the populist strategy, can be constructed in very different ways. In several European countries, the anti-establishment demands have been captured by right-wing populist parties that are articulating in an authoritarian way the rejection of post-democracy. Those movements construct a 'people' through an exclusive ethno-nationalist discourse that excludes migrants, considered as a threat to national iden-tity and prosperity. They advocate a democracy aimed at exclusively defending the interests of those considered 'true nationals'. In the name of recovering democracy, they are in fact calling for restricting it.

I argue that to impede the success of those authoritar-ian movements it is necessary to construct the political frontier in a way that will deepen democracy instead of restricting it. This means deploying a left populist strat-egy whose aim is the constitution of 'a people' constructed through a 'chain of equivalence' among a diversity of democratic struggles around issues concerning exploita-tion, domination, and discrimination. Such a strategy means reasserting the importance of the 'social question', taking account of the increasing fragmentation and diver-sity of the 'workers', but also of the specificity of the vari-ous democratic demands around feminism, antiracism, and LGBTQ+ issues. The objective is the articulation of a transversal 'collective will', a 'people', apt to come to power and establish a new hegemonic formation to foster a process that will radicalize democracy.

Such a process of democratic radicalization engages with the existing political institutions with a view to profoundly transforming them through democratic procedures. It is a strategy that does not aim at a radical break with pluralist liberal democracy and the foundation of a totally new political order. It is therefore clearly different, both from the revolutionary strategy of the 'extreme left' and from the sterile reformism of the social liberals. It is a strategy of 'radical reformism'.

Since publication in 2018, several political forces that I present in the book as following a 'left populist' strategy, like Podemos in Spain, Jean-Luc Mélenchon's La France Insoumise, and the Labour Party under Jeremy Corbyn, have suffered a series of electoral setbacks. Hence the claim in some left sectors that such a project has failed and that it is time to return to more traditional forms of left politics. Those setbacks are undeniable, but it is clearly inadequate to dismiss a political strategy on the sole ground that some of its adherents did not manage to reach their objectives in their first attempt.

Those who draw such a conclusion mistakenly identify the left populist strategy with a 'war of movement'; rather, it is a 'war of position' in which there are always moments of advance and retreat. What's more, when we examine the reasons for the disappointing results of Podemos, the Labour Party, and La France Insoumise, we ascertain that in each case they do badly when they abandon their previous left populist strategy. Indeed, when Podemos, in 2015, and Corbyn and Mélenchon, in 2017, ran left populist campaigns, although they did not win, they obtained very good results. It is only when they followed a different strategy in later elections that their vote began to decline. And when Mélenchon went back to left populism in the 2022 presidential elections, he again did well. This suggests that the left populist strategy is still relevant and should not be abandoned.

To be sure we are no longer in a 'hot' populist moment of high politicization, and the conditions today are clearly very different from the ones that existed before the pandemic. The repeated lockdowns and the forms of control implemented by several neoliberal governments brought to a halt public demonstrations against austerity. In the name of impeding the propagation of the coronavirus, increasingly authoritarian measures were put into place. It is not a particularly propitious moment for organizing popular resistance. However, it would be a mistake to claim that this new situation requires a completely different strategy for the left.

What is important is to recognize the specificity of the current conjuncture. It is characterized by a double challenge: how to deal with the social and economic consequences of the pandemic and how to deal with the climate emergency caused by the effects of global warming. Global warming is only one of the many dimensions of the climate crisis, but it is undoubtedly the most visible, and its impact is directly felt by a great number of people. Scientists have been alerting us to the dramatic consequences of this phenomenon for many years, but they were not heard. However, thanks to the mobilization of the youth, the climate has gained a prominent place in the political agenda. When envisaging a response to the neoliberal offensive, the social and ecological crises, though different, cannot be separated. Even so, to understand the nature of the struggles in which they are inscribed, it is useful to analyze them separately.

In this chapter, I will scrutinize the consequences of the various measures neoliberal governments have implemented to deal with the social and economic consequences of the pandemic. Do they signal a move in the direction of a 'post-neoliberal' horizon, as some suggest, or are we rather seeing the emergence of a new version of neoliberalism better suited to the current predicament?

The response of most governments to the Covid-19 sanitary crisis has been marked by a high level of state intervention. Massive injections of money by the central banks have prevented many business failures and allowed industries to survive without having to lay off workers. While an important part of economic activity has come to an abrupt halt, a catastrophic economic collapse has been avoided thanks to the implementation of diverse forms of subsidies and furlough schemes. The unexpected level of state intervention probably led people to believe it meant a rupture with neoliberal principles. Is this really the case?

Neoliberalism was born to defend society against the 'collectivism' promoted by Marxist and Keynesian theories, and since its origins with the Mont Pelerin Society in 1947, its declared enemy has been the interventionist state, famously presented by Friedrich Hayek as putting societies on 'the road to serfdom'. This approach remained marginal during the years of the post-war welfare state.

After being tested in Chile under the dictatorship of Augusto Pinochet, neoliberalism was able to impose its conception of a free market economy and undertake the dismantling of the welfare state when Margaret Thatcher came to power in 1979 and Ronald Reagan in 1981. As Milton Friedman declared, the moment had come for what had long seemed politically impossible to become 'politically inevitable'.

The neoliberal offensive took advantage of the crisis of the Keynesian economic model in the 1970s, which was caused by the difficulties resulting from a period of stagflation (the increase in inflation accompanied by unemployment), to declare the urgency to drastically change economic strategy. Deciding to break the compromise established between capital and labour and re-establish the prominence of capital, its advocates claimed that the increase in democratic demands and the power acquired by the unions had made society 'ungovernable'. It was high time, as Hayek put it, to 'dethrone politics'.

It is worth underlining that, although heralded as liberating people from the tyranny of the state and opening an era of freedom, neoliberal policies were from the start accompanied by strong repressive measures against their opponents. This is what happened with the miners in Britain and public sector labour unions in the United States. As Andrew Gamble observed, bringing to the fore the significant role of the state in the actual practices of neoliberalism, the strategy was one of 'free economy, strong state'.[3] What had to be curtailed were the redistributive functions of the state and their role in planning the economy; the state's repressive functions had to be

reinforced to defend property rights and secure the working of the free market.

As David Harvey pointed out in *A Brief History of
Neoliberalism*,

> Neoliberalism is in the first instance a theory of politi-
> cal economic practices that proposes that human well-
> being can best be advanced by liberating individual
> entrepreneurial freedoms and skills within an institu-
> tional framework characterized by strong private prop-
> erty rights, free markets and free trade. The role of the
> state is to create and preserve an institutional frame-
> work appropriate to such practices.[4]

In the book, he shows how the turn to neoliberalism since
the 1970s has been accompanied by practices of deregulation, privatization, and withdrawal of the state from many
areas of social provision.

Through the implementation of these practices, the
neoliberal approach succeeded in imposing the idea that
freedom of the market was the condition for the exercise
of individual freedom. Such an assumption became so
ingrained in the common sense that it ended up being
taken for granted. After having been restrained during the
social-democratic consensus of the post-war welfare state,
the ideology of 'possessive individualism' began to constitute the matrix of many social relations.

In Britain it was mobilized by Margaret Thatcher, who
undertook her ideological offensive to disarticulate the
key elements of the social-democratic hegemony under
the banner of 'freedom'. What had been considered social

problems requiring social solutions, like unemployment, were redefined as individual failings, and state intervention was presented as a form of oppression. By heralding the virtues of the free market, Thatcher was able to get the support of many sectors that were attracted by her promise to liberate them from the oppressive power of the state.

As I indicated in *For a Left Populism*, Thatcherism resonated with a wide sector of the popular classes because the bureaucratic way in which many social services were distributed had generated resistance to state intervention. Thatcher's capacity to harness the affects at play in that resistance is what explains her success in implementing neoliberal policies in Britain.

In addition, it is important to realize that a neoliberal regime can adopt a variety of ideological forms for different contexts, while sharing a set of common features. And this is why one should be careful not to mistake a new version of neoliberalism for a rupture. In the case of Thatcherism, neoliberal principles were articulated with neo-conservatism, but when Tony Blair's New Labour came to power in 1997, new forms were established. The key tenets of neoliberalism were articulated with redistributive social-democratic themes to form what Stuart Hall called 'a social-democratic version of neoliberalism'.

Neoliberalism's capacity to adapt to different situations and respond to changing regulations of capitalism has been revealed by the way it incorporates aspects of new countercultural movements, which Luc Boltanski and Eve Chiapello designate as a 'new spirit of capitalism'.[5] The affects at stake in the ideal of self-management, anti-hierarchical exigency, and search for authenticity were put at the service of the development of the post-Fordist networked economy and transformed into new forms of control. As I argued in *Agonistics*, this move is an example of what Antonio Gramsci called 'hegemony through neutralization' or 'passive revolution'.[6] This refers to a situation where demands and affects that challenge a hegemonic order are recuperated and satisfied in a way that neutralizes their subversive potential.

As we have seen, the neoliberal offensive in the 1980s was fundamentally a reaction against the post-war compromise between capital and labour. It was a *reconquista* of the capitalist forces after years in which they had been forced to accept the social and democratic advances made by the working classes. It was a political move to put the state at the service of capital in order to re-establish the conditions for accumulation and restore the power of economic elites. Harvey notes that, while this offensive succeeded in restoring, or creating, the power of economic elites, it was less effective in revitalizing global capital accumulation.

To understand this lack of success, we can turn to Wolfgang Streeck's *Buying Time*.[7] In analyzing the evolution of democratic capitalism since the neoliberal revolution, Streeck helps us grasp why neoliberal policies have not been able to revitalize capital accumulation. Emphasizing the articulation of economic and political factors, he shows how this evolution has been driven by the tensions between two conflicting principles within the regime of democratic capitalism since the end of the Second World War: market justice and social justice.

He presents the development of democratic capitalism as repeated unsuccessful attempts to come to terms with what constitutes its central contradiction: the need to reconcile the logic of capitalist accumulation with democratic institutions, or the interests of capital markets with the interests of the voters. He illustrates the tensions inherent in democratic capitalism, and the limits of public policy in managing them, by the sequence of crises that constitutes the history of wealthy capitalist democracies since the 1970s. The crucial issue was always how to deal with the conflicting requirements of system integration and social integration.

Streeck discerns a three-tiered historical process: the tax state, the debt state, and the consolidation state. Inflation in the 1970s, rising public debt in the 1980s, and the deregulation of private credit in the 1990s in compensation for a first wave of fiscal consolidation and attempts to 'restore sound money' under the pressure of a global haute finance are all expressions of a clash between two diverging sets of normative principles: social justice and market justice. According to him, the contradiction between the interests of the citizens and those of the market have deepened during the latest phase of this development because the transition from the national debt state to the international consolidation state, under the auspices of the European Union, has reinforced the power of the financial markets.

Streeck predicts that, since the capitalism of the consolidation state can no longer produce even the illusion of equitable growth, the paths of capitalism and democracy will part. There is an irresolvable clash between a popular moral economy of the social rights of citizenship and a capitalist economy insisting on allocation according to market justice in line with the requirements of business. And he asserts that 'those who refused to bow to market justice, in a situation where political institutions were economically neutralized, would be left with what used to be described in the 1970s as extra-parliamentary protest'.[8]

Buying Time was published in German in 2013, and the emergence of anti-establishment protest movements since then could be interpreted as according with Streeck's prognosis. The populist moment I analysed in *For a Left Populism* was in many respects the consequence of the crisis of democratic capitalism, especially its incapacity to sustain its hegemony in the context of the austerity policies of the consolidation state dictated by the financial markets. This explains the recourse to authoritarian and repressive measures to secure compliance to a social order that was beginning to be resisted by an increasing number of citizens. Such an authoritarian turn has taken place in countries where, when the neoliberal strategy of 'nudging' people to act according to the requirements of capital failed, popular resistance was crushed by the police, as was the case in France with the Gilets Jaunes.

In circumstances in which the legitimacy of the system has been undermined, it is reasonable to expect the resistance to authoritarian measures to grow and the level of social antagonism to increase. This was indeed the view I defended in *For a Left Populism*, where I visualized a 'return of the political' that would take the form of a struggle between right-wing populism and left populism.

This was of course before the current pandemic. As I

noted earlier, today we are faced with the double crisis of the climate emergency and the economic and social consequences of a sanitary one. There is no doubt that the emergence of the coronavirus and its spread across the planet have been facilitated by the destruction of the environment, destruction that has been accelerated and intensified by financial capitalism. Decades of neoliberal austerity policies have destroyed the public services of many countries, which found themselves unprepared in the face of the pandemic.

For these reasons, the coronavirus validates the theses of the progressive camp, and many expect that it signals the end of the hegemony of neoliberal capitalism. They think that since Covid-19 has exacerbated existing inequalities and crises, once normality is re-established the popular struggles will resume with a renewed vigour. They might be right, but I am afraid that, instead of intensifying the crisis of legitimacy of neoliberalism, the pandemic might give it a new lease on life.

What leads me to envisage such a possibility is the surmise that the pandemic has generated affects that are linked to a strong need for security and a demand for protection. I draw this hypothesis from reading Karl Polanyi. In his book *The Great Transformation*, he revealed how society in the 1930s, imperilled by the dislocation caused by advances in commodification, reacted with a counter-movement that readapted the economy to social needs.[9] He also observed that the resistance to this dislocation did not necessarily take a democratic form. Indeed, it led not just to Roosevelt's New Deal but also to fascism and Stalinism.

Polanyi's idea of a counter-movement has gained currency in recent years to explain the global growth of contemporary social movements resisting neoliberalism. I find this dimension of his work illuminating, but I want to refer to another one that I find particularly relevant in the present conjuncture: the importance he attributes to the element of self-protection. He shows that when societies experience serious disturbances in their modes of life, the need for protection becomes the central demand, and people are likely to follow those who they feel can best provide it.

We find ourselves in an analogous situation. The circumstances are of course different, but there is no doubt that the pandemic has had a profound affective impact on large sectors of the population. While the poorest and those in precarious jobs have certainly been most affected, the disruption brought about by the pandemic has given rise among many different sectors to a general feeling of vulnerability that expresses a desire for security and protection.

This desire can be addressed in different ways, progressively or regressively. It can benefit right-wing populists if they are able to convince people that security requires adopting a view of sovereignty in terms of exclusive nationalism. And they are clearly busy promoting such a view. Claiming to be the voice of the people, they accuse the neoliberal elites and their politics of globalization of being responsible for the crisis because they abandon national sovereignty and defend free trade. The right-wing anti-establishment discourse, the call to recover sovereignty, and the rejection of the rule of transnational corporations are well received and resonate with the popular sectors.

Nevertheless, in contrast to what I wrote in *For a Left Populism*, in the current conjuncture I do not think that right-wing populists should always be seen as the principal opponent. To be sure, in certain countries they represent a danger for democracy, but it is a mistake to focus all our energies on fighting them at the cost of neglecting other adversaries. I am, for instance, particularly concerned by the fact that this feeling of vulnerability is being exploited by neoliberal governments to foster the development of a neoliberal version of techno-authoritarianism, presented as the best way to provide security and protection. With innovative digital technologies like the QR code they are trying to reinforce their power and restore their legitimacy.

In no way do I want to support the claim made by Giorgio Agamben and others who see the pandemic as having been engineered with the aim of controlling the population. But there is no doubt that neoliberals have been attempting to turn it to their advantage. We saw a sign of this early on, in the promotion of a techno-security response to the sanitary crisis, which asserted that the solution consisted in procuring apps to control the health of the population. This opened the way for digital giants to establish themselves as the agents of a fully computer-ized health policy.

The pandemic has clearly provided a great opportunity for the big tech companies that, thanks to the periods of confinement, have realized unexpected gains. Now their ambition is to extend their control to a variety of other domains. This could lead to the 'Screen New Deal' envisaged by Naomi Klein, something resembling a coherent 'Pandemic Shock Doctrine' that would be placed in the hands of companies like Amazon, Google, and Apple to whom important decisions about how to organize our life are outsourced, allowing them to receive public funds while eliminating all democratic control.[10]

At a moment when their main objective is to impede the return of political antagonism after the 'pause' of the pandemic, the neoliberal elites are aware of the need to answer the demands for protection that it has awoken. And they are actively encouraging digital forms of protection. This has already produced effects, since many people are currently ready to accept digital forms of control that they used to oppose. While this process of the digitalization of social control had no doubt already begun, the pandemic intensified and entrenched already existing trends. The pandemic will probably be seen as a key moment in the evolution towards a digital capitalism that fosters post-democratic forms of techno-authoritarianism that remain immune from democratic control.

This authoritarian digital neoliberalism is being legitimized by the fashionable 'technological solutionism' that Evgeny Morozov analyzed. Already in 2013, in his book *To Save Everything, Click Here*, he warned against the ideology of solutionism promoted by Silicon Valley according to which all problems, even political ones, have a technological solution.[11] Such an approach, says Morozov, has been reinforced by the growth of the internet, which has allowed the solutionists to expand the scope of their interventions. In his view, the danger lies in simplifying problems to procure immediate results that do not allow us to examine intellectually complex and more demanding projects of reform.

I see in this solutionism a technological version of the post-political conception that became dominant during the 1990s. By deploying digital technologies, solutionists advocate post-ideological measures, and this allows them to avoid politics. Their belief that digital platforms can provide a foundation for the political order clearly chimes with the claim of third-way politicians that political antagonisms have been overcome and that left and right are 'zombie categories'.

Some neoliberals hope that this digital capitalism, enhanced by the remarkable developments of artificial intelligence, will provide the solution to the crisis of accumulation that is afflicting capitalism. They see the digitalization of numerous activities in a variety of domains – work, education, health, and others – as a way of reducing the costs of production, and they are convinced it will have a profound impact on the dynamics of capitalism, announcing the beginning of a new era. They also claim that the development of a 'green capitalism' and the promotion of geo-engineering represent the solution to the problem of global warming, and they are eager to take advantage of the field of opportunities presented by the climate emergency.

We must be aware that the pursuit of such projects could give neoliberalism a new possibility of 'buying time'. To be sure, the contradictions between the demands of the market and those of the citizens would remain, and the incompatibility between capitalism and democracy would not disappear, but this new form of digital post-politics would represent a serious setback for the forces of democracy.

2
Politics and Affects

Faced with attempts, by both the far right and neoliberal elites, to take advantage of the affects caused by the pandemic to impose an authoritarian model, it is imperative for the left to address the demand for security and protection. This represents a challenge because the rationalist framework that often informs left politics constitutes an obstacle to acknowledging the importance of affects. Indeed, everything that has to do with the realm of emotions, with affective attachments, is deemed inconsistent with the advance of progress under the guide of Reason. This is particularly marked in the 'globalist' left that, having adopted the neoliberal world view that postulates the end of the adversarial model of politics, conceives moral progress as the creation of a borderless world where everything can move freely and without hindrance, a world without antagonisms, where politics is a domain of rational decisions made by experts. This segment of the left is thereby suspicious of the desire for security, which it regards as being of a conservative nature, conflicting with the 'progressive' and cosmopolitan values it cherishes.

How to overcome this reluctance and formulate the democratic project in a way that recognizes the importance of affects? This question has been at the centre of my reflexion since *Hegemony and Socialist Strategy*.[1] It is at the core of my critique of Jürgen Habermas and other theorists of deliberative democracy, who uphold a rationalist conception that leaves no space for passions and affective forms of identification. In their view, the development of modern society has established the conditions for a 'deliberative democracy', in which decisions on matters of common concern should result from the free and unconstrained public deliberation of all. They see politics as the field in which a rational consensus will be established through the free exercise of public reason (John Rawls) or under the conditions of undistorted communication (Habermas). Passions are erased from the realm of politics, which is reduced to a field of competing interests under the constraints of morality. By postulating an ideal of rational consensus, they partake in what Oliver Marchart calls the 'associative view' of the political, a view I have criticized for denying the partisan nature of politics and the ever-present possibility of antagonism.[2]

I have also exposed how such a perspective is responsible for the inadequate way in which most currents of democratic theory envisage the nature of the allegiance to democracy. They are incapable of recognizing that it is through identification – that is, affects – one can create allegiance to democratic institutions. Many democratic theorists think that what is needed to secure the future of liberal democratic institutions are rational grounds. For Habermas it is a question of legitimacy whose central issue lies in finding a way to guarantee that decisions taken by democratic institutions represent an impartial standpoint expressing the interests of all. He wants to make the type of rationality at work in communicative action and public reason the main motivation for democratic citizens and the basis of their allegiance to democratic institutions.

Taking issue with this rationalist conception, I have argued that what is really at stake in the allegiance to those institutions is a matter not of rational justification but of availability of forms of identification and multiple practices that make possible the creation of democratic citizens. An approach privileging rationality leaves aside a central element, which is the crucial role played by passions and affects in securing allegiance to democratic values.

It is not by providing arguments about the rationality embodied in liberal democratic institutions that one can contribute to the creation of democratic citizens, but by multiplying the discourses, the institutions, and the forms of life that foster identification with democratic values. The question at stake is one not of rationality but of common affects.

Addressing the issue of allegiance to democracy from that angle, we can see that, by emphasizing the arguments needed to secure the legitimacy of its institutions, political theorists have been asking the wrong question. Democracy does not require a theory of truth and notions like unconditionality and universal validity; it is more in the nature of what Ludwig Wittgenstein likens to 'a passionate commitment to a system of reference'.[3] Allegiance to democracy is a question of identification with democratic values, and this is a complex process in which affects play a crucial role.

To grasp the reasons for the entanglement between the democratic project and the rationalist approach, we need to go back to the Enlightenment. This is a question I already discussed in *The Democratic Paradox*, and it is worth revisiting some of the arguments developed in that book because they are relevant for understanding our current predicament.[4]

For instance, important insights can be gained by following the perspective of Pierre Saint-Amand, who, in *The Laws of Hostility*, proposes a political anthropology of the Enlightenment that sheds light on its blind spots.[5] He shows how, in their attempt to ground politics on reason, the *philosophes* of the Enlightenment were led to present an optimistic view of sociability, seeing violence as an archaic phenomenon that does not belong to human nature. They believed that antagonistic and violent forms of behaviour, everything that was the manifestation of hostility, could be eradicated thanks to the progress of exchange and the development of sociability.

Scrutinizing this optimistic view through the mimetic theory developed by René Girard, Saint-Amand avers that it acknowledges only one side of what constitutes the dynamics of imitation. It is based on a conception of human exchange aimed exclusively at the realization of the good, and it only acknowledges one part of the mimetic aspects, those linked to empathy. For Girard, however, it is vital to recognize the ambivalent nature of the concept of imitation and the conflictual nature of mimesis – the fact that the very movement that brings people together in their common desire for the same object is also at the origin of their antagonism. Reciprocity and hostility cannot be dissociated, and the social order will always be threatened by violence.

Saint-Amand points out that it was the very nature of their humanistic project that led the authors of the *Encyclopédie* to defend a flawed, idealized view of sociability. It is because they wanted to ground the autonomy of the social and secure equality among human beings that they denied the negative side of exchange, in particular its dissociating impulse. He shows that this denial was the very condition for the fiction of a social contract from which violence and hostility were to be eliminated and where reciprocity could take the form of transparent communication among participants.

Such a view is harmful for democratic politics, because democratic politics cannot be enhanced by denying the violence inherent in sociability – violence that no contract can eliminate since it is a component of sociability. On the contrary, only by acknowledging the contradictory drives set to work by social exchange is it possible to grasp the practices and institutions necessary to secure democratic order.

Not surprisingly, the humanistic perspective of the *philosophes* cannot envisage a positive role for affects and passions, which are seen as 'irrational' forces, archaic remnants of an age where reason had not yet reached its full deployment. Although the conception of the modern individual as guided by reason, which is at the centre of the doctrine of the *philosophes*, was expressed in diverse ways according to the different national traditions of the Enlightenment, all share the view that a radical opposition between reason and passion exists and that affects are to be kept at bay because they constitute an obstacle to the pursuit of rational conduct. This explains why the rich reflexion on passions that we find in many seventeenth-century philosophers like Pascal, Spinoza, and Hobbes was interrupted by the self-proclaimed Age of Reason in the eighteenth century.

It is interesting to note that, despite the negative way they were seen by Enlightenment thinkers, not all passions suffered the same fate. In his book *The Passions and the Interests: Political Arguments for Capitalism before Its Triumph*, Albert Hirschman reconstructs the intellectual climate of the seventeenth and eighteenth centuries.[6] He discusses the works of Montesquieu, James Steuart, and Adam Smith to indicate how a passion that used to be condemned as the sin of avarice, like the pursuit of material interest, was re-signified in a positive way in terms of 'interests' and assigned the role of containing the unruly and destructive passions of man. And he argues that this move from passions to interests played a significant role in the rise of capitalism.

What is particularly relevant for my purpose is the link that was established between the democratic project and the rationalist perspective. Democratic values were seen as grounded on the advances of rationality, and the claim that they had to be defended against the interference of affects became so central that the authors who tried to bring to light the limits of Enlightenment rationalism and who insisted that allegiance to democracy could not be guaranteed by reason alone were perceived as defending a conservative position. They were accused of undermining the very basis of the democratic project.

This is where we probably see the origin of the widespread view that the left must self-identify as rational and that it should shun the passions. Such a conception is still found today among political theorists. For example, in his book *The Philosophical Discourse of Modernity*, Habermas accuses critics of modern reason like Michel Foucault of promoting views inimical to the democratic tradition and jeopardizing the very basis of democracy.[7]

For questioning the thesis that the defence of democracy must be based on a rationalist perspective that disqualifies the role of affect, Hans Blumenberg's *The Legitimacy of the Modern Age* provides inspiration.[8] Here Blumenberg provides us with invaluable insights to refute the claim that the critique of Enlightenment rationalism constitutes a threat to the modern democratic project. In his discussion of Karl Löwith's thesis that the idea of progress is a secularized version of Christian eschatology, Blumenberg argues that the modern age possesses a truly novel quality in the form of the idea of 'self-assertion'. Such an idea emerges as a response to the situation created by scholastic theology's decline into 'theological absolutism', a set of ideas associated with belief in an omnipotent and completely free God.

In the face of this theological absolutism, which made the world completely contingent, the only solution, writes Blumenberg, was the affirmation of human reason as a measure of order and source of value. Against what theorists of secularization maintain, he asserts that there is a genuine break, although it coexists with a certain continuity. But it is a continuity of problems, not of solutions. According to him:

> What mainly occurred in the process that is interpreted as secularization, at least (so far) in all but a few recognizable and specific instances should be described not as the *transposition* of authentically theological contents into secularized alienation from their origin but rather as the *reoccupation* of answer positions that had become vacant and whose corresponding questions could not be eliminated.[9]

As Richard Rorty suggests, this can be interpreted in a way that would allow us to distinguish what is truly modern: the idea of 'self-assertion' (identified with the political project) as distinct from the idea of 'self-grounding' (the epistemological project).[10] The latter is merely a 'reoccupation' of a medieval position. It is an attempt to give a modern answer to a premodern question instead of abandoning it, as a rationality conscious of its limits would have done. Following Rorty, we could therefore be entitled to conclude that it is when modern reason acknowledges its limits and accepts the impossibility of total control and final harmony that it frees itself from its premodern heritage. The illusion of Reason providing itself with its own foundations, which accompanied the labour of liberation from theology, may thus be called into question. However, this does not necessarily undermine the democratic project.

I regard this as a crucial move, because the belief in the existence of a necessary link between the two sides of the Enlightenment, the political and the epistemological, explains the attachment of the left to an impoverished view of rationality that excludes affects. Once we accept that there is no necessary relation between the two projects, the political and the epistemological, we are in a condition to defend the democratic political project while abandoning the notion that it must be based on rationalism, understood as a form of rationality free from affects.

Taking my bearing from such an approach, I have elaborated an 'agonistic' conception of democracy that envisages the democratic project without resorting to the universal dictates of reason.[11] Detaching democracy from the problematic of individualism and highlighting the crucial role played by affects in the construction of political identities, I have underlined both the collective and the partisan character of political action. One of the weakest points of liberal democratic theories is their incapacity to apprehend the collective nature of political identities and their affective dimension. I take this incapacity to be the consequence of these theories' image of the individual, which is presented as acting in the field of politics either in pursuit of her own interests or because of abstract moral principles. This impedes asking what I take to be one of the key questions for politics: How are collective forms of identification created, and what part do affects/passions play in this process?

Contrary to the view that democracy consists in enacting procedures for reaching an inclusive consensus, which requires eliminating passions from the political sphere, the agonistic view conceives democratic politics as the establishment of institutions that allow for a transformation of antagonism into agonism – that is, an agonistic expression of dissensus. What is important is that conflict, when it arises, takes the form not of an 'antagonism' (struggle between enemies) but of an 'agonism' (struggle between adversaries). The agonistic confrontation is different from the antagonistic one, not because it allows for a possible consensus, but because the opponent is considered not an enemy to be destroyed but an adversary whose existence is perceived as legitimate.

The challenge for democracy, therefore, is to establish the we/they distinction, which is constitutive of politics, in a way that is compatible with the recognition of pluralism. As Marcel Mauss felicitously put it, its aim is to 'oppose without killing each other'. What is at stake in the agonistic struggle is the configuration of power relations that structure a social order and the type of hegemony they construct. It is a confrontation between conflicting hegemonic projects that can never be reconciled rationally. Unlike the rationalist models that want to keep passions out of politics, the agonistic perspective takes account of the crucial role they play in the constitution of political identities. Furthermore, it sees the public sphere as the battlefield where passions are mobilized through the confrontation of hegemonic projects, with no possibility of a final reconciliation.

The critique of rationalism, far from being limited to a philosophical dispute, has direct political relevance, and I have often inscribed my reflexion in specific political conjunctures. For instance, in *On the Political*, scrutinizing the model of the 'third way', I took issue with its claim that the adversarial type of politics had become obsolete and that it was now necessary to think 'beyond right and left' in view of reaching a consensus at the centre.[12] I brought to light how, by negating the partisan character of political action, such a 'post-political' conception impeded an agonistic debate aimed at mobilizing affects around democratic projects. I warned that this was creating a favourable terrain for right-wing populist parties that claimed to be giving back to the people the voice that had been confiscated by the establishment elites.

To counter the rise of 'post-politics', I made a case for reaffirming the left/right opposition and for relinquishing the consensual politics of the 'third way', which was depriving citizens of the possibility of a real choice between democratic alternatives. Alas, in the following years the rise of right-wing populism confirmed the prognosis I made in 2005. This rise also confirmed that the neglect of affects represents an obstacle in the attempts by the rationalist left to rally support for their policies. It is why they lack the mobilizing power of far-right movements who do not shy away from stirring passions and appealing to the register of emotions.

I contend that in the current conjuncture, characterized by an increasing disaffection with democracy and marked by a worrying level of abstention, highlighting the partisan nature of politics and the centrality of affects is essential. This is the condition for reaching all those who have deserted political parties because they feel that their concerns are ignored and that elections do not offer real alternatives.

People need to feel that by engaging in politics they are given a voice, that they are empowered. Among the affects disdained by the globalist left, those expressing demands for sovereignty, protection, and security are paramount, and abandoning them to the right would be a serious political mistake. It prevents the elaboration of a political project capable of resonating with the demands of the popular classes. Instead of dismissing those demands, the task is to articulate them with democratic values to offer forms of identification in which the desire for protection is secured in an egalitarian way.

While I have always been critical of the rationalism of the left, I feel that in the current conjuncture, to resist the authoritarian offensive there is a real urgency to discard it because it prevents us from understanding the importance of mobilizing the affects required to construct a popular movement. The success of such a movement depends on its capacity to recognize the affective dimension at play in the construction of collective forms of identification. To generate adhesion, it needs to convey affects that resonate with people's concerns and personal experiences.

It is dispiriting to see so many radicals and socialists dedicating all their energy to the elaboration of policies and programmes they are convinced people will accept by virtue of their superior rationality, while neglecting to ask how to generate the affects that will give force to those policies. This is no doubt thanks to their belief in the existence of a 'scientific socialism', an idea that has played an important role in the diffusion of a rationalist conception of politics among significant sectors of the left.

Today some people are still clinging to an orthodox version of historical materialism that sees socialism as the necessary outcome of a contradiction between forces of production and relations of production. They are adamant that their conception of history, based on 'scientific grounds', has a privileged access to truth that trumps the 'ideological' positions of their opponents, and they see their role as explaining the road to follow to reach the socialist objective determined by the course of history. Since they are certain that they know what is good for the people, they do not see the need to wonder about the people's real aspirations. Even among those who do not embrace such a rationalist conception, many are convinced that their message should only be directed to the intellect and that the condition for winning is to offer a clearly avowed socialist programme.

To bring about a new hegemony aimed at defending and deepening democracy requires much more than a well-elaborated programme. As Pierre Bourdieu reminds us, there is no intrinsic force to true ideas. Rational arguments are not sufficient, and what drives people to struggle is not the trust in the existence of a 'law of history' leading to socialism. People fight against various forms of domination they experience in their daily life, not for the realization of abstract ideas. Abstract ideas, although they might be important in elaborating theories, are not what make people act politically and mobilize their energies, because they do not convey the affective force that is indispensable for acquiring real power. What moves people to act are affects and the identifications in which those affects are inscribed.

It is essential to distinguish between social theory and political praxis. While socialist principles can provide useful theoretical guidelines to envisage the construction of egalitarian societies, when it comes to political praxis, I am convinced it is not by appealing to socialism that it is possible to mobilize passions and generate the common affects around which a progressive collective will can crystallize.

In our societies, the 'signifier' of socialism has, for a multiplicity of reasons, lost the mobilizing power that it might have had in the past. As testified by popular mobilizations like the Indignados in Spain, the diversity of Occupy movements in the US and worldwide, Nuit Debout and the Gilets Jaunes in France, not to mention the various Arab Spring revolts, the rallying cry of the 'movements of the squares' was a demand not for socialism but for 'real democracy'. More recently, during the mass protests that sprang up around the globe in reaction to the killing of George Floyd, it is under the banner of the Black Lives Matter movement that people have gathered and that anti-racism consciousness has been raised.

The urgencies of all these different mobilizations had to do with social justice and equality, but they did not formulate their demands in a socialist vocabulary with which they did not identify. A political project needs to speak to people based on their lived experiences and concrete aspirations. It must stem from their actual conditions and designate adversaries that they can identify. It is always around specific demands that people can be politicized, and an abstract anti-capitalist rhetoric does not resonate with many of the groups whose interests the radicals aim to represent.

It is not my intention to deny that there is necessarily an 'anti-capitalist' dimension in the struggle for the radicalization of democracy. It is undeniable that such a process will require putting an end to many forms of domination whose origin lies in the capitalist mode of production. And if we accept, as proposed in *Hegemony and Socialist Strategy*, to reformulate socialism in terms of a radicalization of democracy, it is indeed possible to present it as the aim of the egalitarian struggle. Still, it is not in the name of anti-capitalism or socialism that most progressive struggles are conducted today, but in the name of equality and social justice, and they are often conceived as democratic struggles.

3
Affects, Identity, and Identification

My argument so far has been that the outcome of the sanitary and ecological crises could herald a neoliberal consolidation or move us towards the construction of a more democratic society. I have warned that, given the neoliberal attempt to harness the need for protection and security generated by the Covid-19 pandemic to install an authoritarian digital model and promote a 'green capitalism', the neglect of affects might prevent left forces from grasping the challenge they are facing.

The question I will address in this chapter is how to apprehend the role of affects in the constitution of political identities. This will show that, contrary to how it is sometimes interpreted, my critique of rationalism is in no way a rejection of the role of rationality and a defence of a sort of 'irrationalism'. Nor is it a call to oppose reason to passion and advocate a politics driven by passion at the expense of reason.

Recently, emotions and affects have become a fashionable topic among philosophers and people working in the social sciences and humanities. I will first specify my position with respect to the current discussion of what has been called the 'affective turn'. The affective turn encompasses a heterogeneous body of work among which it is not easy to find 'family resemblances', because the theorists who are sometimes put under this umbrella come from a variety of approaches which are difficult to reconcile. They disagree on the very meaning of the terms 'affects' and 'emotions', not to mention their relation. Some of them are influenced by Gilles Deleuze and Félix Guattari, others by the neurosciences, others by a variety of constructivist schools. Several of these studies provide valuable insights, but since their focus is different from mine, it is necessary to clarify the differences between my approach and theirs.

My reflexion concerns a certain type of affects, those I call 'passions'. By 'passions' I designate the *common* affects that are at stake in the political domain in the formation of we/they forms of identification. From the perspective I advocate, it is essential to distinguish passions from emotions. In the political domain, we are always dealing with collective identities, something that the term 'emotions' does not adequately convey because emotions are usually attached to individuals. In the field of politics, speaking of common affects and 'passions' is more appropriate to suggest a confrontation between collective political identities.

Bringing together the discursive anti-essentialist perspective elaborated in *Hegemony and Socialist Strategy* and some fundamental insights of psychoanalysis should allow us to connect affects and reason in the process of identification and envisage how affects can be mobilized in the construction of a collective will. This requires adopting a theoretical approach according to which the problem of identity is a question not of people discovering or recognizing their true, essential identity, but of constructing it. An important dimension of politics is the construction of political identities through a process of identification, a process that always entails an affective dimension, what Freud calls a libidinal investment.

Freud is central for my reflexion on affects. He has been a constant reference in my work, and has deeply influenced my thinking of the political. I have often emphasized how his critique of the unified character of the subject and his claim that the human mind is necessarily subject to division between two systems, one of which is not and cannot be conscious, is crucial for a critique of the rationalist perspective. Indeed, it obliges us to abandon one of the keys tenets of rationalist philosophy, namely the subject as a rational, transparent entity able to confer a homogeneous meaning on the totality of their conduct. The claim of psychoanalysis that there are no essential identities but only forms of identification is at the centre of the anti-essentialist approach. This stipulates that the history of the subject is the history of their identifications, beyond which there is no concealed identity to be rescued. Any identity, therefore, is constructed through a variety of identifications with socially available objects as images and signifiers.

In *For a Left Populism*, discussing the relevance of Freud's work for envisaging the construction of a 'people', I stressed the importance of his thesis that the social link is a libidinal link and that affects play a crucial role in processes of collective identification. What is at stake in collective identification for Freud is the libidinal organization of groups, and assuming a collective identity is about affective libidinal bonds. As he stated in *Group Psychology and the Analysis of the Ego*, 'A group is clearly held together by a power of some kind: and to what power could this feat be better ascribed than to Eros, which holds together everything in the world.'[1]

Affective libidinal energy is malleable and capable of different investments. It is susceptible of being transferred along a variety of different representations and can be oriented in multiple directions, producing diverse forms of identification. This point is essential for understanding the work of the hegemonic operation since it requires realizing that different forms of politics can foster different affective libidinal attachments.

We can expand these reflexions thanks to advances made in the field of psychoanalysis by theorists influenced by Jacques Lacan, who developed and enriched several aspects of Freud's work. Many of these advances have important implications for political analysis and are particularly relevant for the argument I want to make in this chapter.

I aim to highlight the role played by affects in the constitution of political identities, and I see the concept of identification as key in addressing this question. Yannis Stavrakakis has made an invaluable contribution in this field. He suggests that a blend of discourse theory and psychoanalysis can provide a promising approach to the question of identity and identification. He deems such an approach to be especially appropriate for exploring 'what makes people collectively identify with particular identity formations, and what implications such identifications entail'.[2]

In his view, while Freud had brought to light 'the dimension of passion, of affective attachment, and libidinal investment, something which presupposes the *energetics of the body*', it is thanks to Lacan that the question of identification can be posed adequately.[3] For Freud, identification refers to the mechanism through which subjectivity is constituted and indicates that the personality is constituted through a series of identifications. Lacan, notes Stavrakakis, develops this insight by distinguishing between different types of identification (imaginary, symbolic, with a symptom) and further highlighting the negative (alienating) horizon of such operations. Although constitutive of subjectivity, identification cannot result in a stable subjective identity.

In other words, a full identity is ultimately impossible because the divided subject meets a lack where it seeks fullness and identity. This is the so-called big Other, our socio-political world, the reservoir of objects with which we identify to resolve subjective tensions, which is also inherently lacking.

In consequence, the subject is always attempting to cover up its constitutive lack through continuous and partial identifications with ultimately incomplete objects. The partiality and incompleteness of these identifications do not negate their everyday value for human life and politics, unless one remains trapped with some sort of obsolete rationalistic utopianism. This is where we should see the relevance of the concept of identification for social and political analysis: 'Since the objects of identification in adult life include political ideologies and other socially constructed objects, the process of identification is revealed as constitutive of socio-political life. It is not identity which is constitutive but identification as such; instead of identity politics we should speak of identification politics.'[4]

Yet what makes such partial identification processes appealing apart from their occasional semblance of consistency? Stavrakakis also argues that Lacan's concept of *jouissance* is his decisive contribution to psychoanalysis. By highlighting the dual nature of identification (discursive and affective, symbolic and libidinal), Lacan allows us to successfully address the question of socio-political identification and identity formation, suggesting that support for particular identifications is partially rooted in the *jouissance* of the body. According to Lacanian theory, what is at stake in these fields 'is not only symbolic coherence and discursive closure but also *enjoyment*, the *jouissance* animating human desire'.[5]

There are accordingly two sides at play in the process of identification. It should be conceived as a signifying practice that includes both a cognitive/representational and an affective dimension, an idea but also an affect – that is, the libidinal force that this signification acquires and that will give it its *force*. It is when the junction between ideas and affects takes place that ideas acquire power. To approach the socio-political field, therefore, one has to proceed from a double source: the order of the signifier (the symbolic) and the order of affect, of jouissance.

Taking the example of national identity, Stavrakakis shows that, although contemporary research envisages the nation as a modern social and political construction and emphasizes the constructed character of national identity, theorists of nationalism are usually not able to explain the longevity, sustained hegemonic appeal and *force* of national identification.[6] Therefore, their critique of nationalism remains at a superficial level. He asserts that to understand the longevity of national identification and the emotional power of nationalism, Lacan's dialectics of *jouissance* offers a more adequate theoretical framework. It reveals that the symbolic aspect of national identification is not sufficient and that 'the mobilization of symbolic resources has to be coupled with an affective investment grounded in the body for national identity to emerge'.[7] The discursive dimension, while no doubt important, is not enough, and the mechanism most effective in structuring subjectivity is not primarily symbolic but linked to the real of *jouissance*; in other words, it is of a libidinal nature.

According to Stavrakakis, interrogating the question of European identity from this perspective allows us to apprehend the reasons for its lack of success. In his view, the different attempts to promote European identity through policies and educational programmes have failed to produce a salient popular identification with the European Union because, by focusing exclusively on institutional arrangements and passionless ideals, 'they have neglected the crucial role of affect and passion in this process'. When the libidinal/affective dimension of identification is missing, he concludes, 'identifications cannot acquire any salience or deep hegemonic appeal'.[8]

As a matter of fact, the lack of an affective dimension in the European project is inscribed in its very conception. Jean Monnet and Robert Schuman, promoting the creation of the coal and steel economy after the Second World War, insisted on the need to base institutions on a rational policy in order to keep them free from popular passions. Although their fear of passions might be understandable owing to the circumstances, it has had negative consequences for the further evolution of the European Union, and may have contributed to it becoming a bureaucratic neoliberal project impervious to the concerns of its citizens.

By grasping what is at stake in the process of identification, the difficulties the left encounters in the hegemonic struggle are brought to light. The belief that one should only use rational arguments and avoid appealing to affects leads to policies with which people cannot identify because they do not recognize in them their own problems, frustrations, and demands. The left spends lots of energy on the elaboration of programmes and on enumerating the great policies that it will implement once in power, but the question it rarely asks is how to get there, how to make people *desire* those policies, as if good policies were enough to automatically generate adhesion without the necessity of activating the affective dimension that will produce identification and spur political engagement. Policies that neglect to address those affects are unlikely to find resonance among the people.

There is another way in which the rationalist approach prevents understanding the nature of hegemonic political struggle. It is also related to the failure to apprehend the dynamics of identification, but this time it is due to an essentialist conception that ascribes certain affects to a determinate category of persons. We can see it, for instance, in the refusal to speak with people who vote for far-right parties with the claim that they are moved by resentment, an affect that needs to be condemned. This is the argument that some sectors of the left in France have used to criticize the attempts of La France Insoumise to engage with followers of Marine Le Pen who come from the popular classes. Clearly, resentment is an affect that has no place in progressive politics, but it should not be ascribed to some individuals as an inherent characteristic of their psychological make-up, thereby claiming that the effort to transform them by generating another affect is in vain.

In truth, resentment is not something people are born with; it always comes from a reaction of anger against a specific situation in which the individual feels to be the victim of some wrong. This anger can be transformed into resentment if the wrong is not offered a perspective of reparation. When we scrutinize the nature of the wrong, we realize it may be possible to address it so that the anger it provokes will not lead to resentment. Indeed, on many occasions specific groups such as migrants are rejected because people are led to perceive them as responsible for the deterioration of their conditions of existence, as the 'them' that impedes the full realization of their rights. This is how right-wing discourse encourages resentment against migrants, who are constructed as the enemy whose presence is responsible for their wrongs.

Take the example of Donald Trump. It is clear his

discourse aims to foster an us/them confrontation that mobilizes white working-class anger, converting it into resentment against minorities and the enlightened elites who champion them. This resentment is the product of a discursive articulation of anger caused by a wrong that could have been articulated differently to construct an us/them aimed at creating another type of identification. This was the type fostered by Bernie Sanders. His discourse offered the working class hope that their situation could be improved through the struggle for social justice. It is interesting here to remember how Emile Durkheim, in his study of socialism, identified the mechanism leading from anger to hope as the origin of the socialist movement at the dawn of the industrial revolution.

The refusal of the rationalist left to engage with the affective dimension of politics explains why so many left parties are unable to connect with the popular classes. This is not a new phenomenon. In his book *Heritage of Our Times*, Ernst Bloch, referring to the situation in Germany in the 1930s, argued that Marxists tended to downplay hunger and the need for security, home, community, and other forms of attachment, which fascism addressed with more success than the left.[9] Hitler's appeal, according to Bloch, was due to his ability to absorb the frustrated demands that existed within German society, energies which could have been positively transformed but were directed towards a politics of hate.

Today there is a tendency among certain sectors of the left to reduce the diversity of right-wing movements to the expression of a neo-fascist threat that should be countered through ostracism and moral condemnation. For this reason, they do not see the importance of trying to understand why people are attracted to such parties. In line with the rationalist framework prevalent in their ranks, the emergence of those movements is perceived as 'the return of the brown plague', as proceeding from the 'irrational' impulses of the masses. In their view, those who support such parties are irredeemable, affected by a sort of incurable 'moral disease' and moved by atavistic passions. Therefore, those who seek to understand the grounds for the success of those parties in order to design ways to counter them and offer different forms of identification for their affects are accused of 'pandering to the extreme right'.

In countries where authoritarian parties of the right are attracting an increasing number of people, such an approach leads to impotence in envisaging how to arrest their growth. Moreover, discarding *a priori* the popular sectors that have been seduced by right-wing demagogues on the grounds that they are intrinsically sexist, racist, and homophobic is clearly at odds with the very purpose of a strategy whose objective is the construction of a popular progressive movement. Of course, the strategy to fight the far right cannot concentrate all its efforts on those sectors, but it cannot eschew seeking to apprehend the nature of the affects that are at play in adhering to those parties.

Addressing the conditions that cause the relations of domination at the origin of the wrong and offering a democratic project that endeavours to eliminate them, a left populist strategy aims to draw the us/them opposition in a way that does not foment resentment but seeks to generate affects towards social justice. At issue here is hegemonic struggle, which is never a purely rational operation of presenting arguments and scientific data to convince people. Hegemonic struggle always deals with identifications that have an important affective dimension. Here we should listen to Spinoza, who told us that the only way to displace an affect was to produce a stronger one.

This is not the first time I refer to Spinoza in my writings with respect to the importance of affects in politics. I would like to specify which aspects of his thought I find especially relevant for my argument. To be sure, Spinoza was ultimately a rationalist, but we can find in his work many valuable insights for elaborating a non-rationalist conception of politics. The affinity between Spinoza's notion of *conatus* and Freud's notion of libido has often been noted. Like Freud, Spinoza believes that desire makes people act, and affects make them act in a certain way. He understood that for ideas to acquire power, it is necessary that they reach people at the affective level, that they acquire, in Freudian terms, a libidinal force.

There are other points of convergence between Spinoza and Freud. Distinguishing between affection (*affectio*) and affect (*affectus*), Spinoza states that when affected by something exterior, the conatus experiences affects that will make it desire something and move it to act accordingly. According to Frédéric Lordon, whose reading of Spinoza I find particularly stimulating, the notion of 'affection', which results as much from ideas as from material determinations, allows us to transcend the antinomy between matter and ideas. He points out that, for Spinoza, politics is an *ars affectandi* that aims to produce ideas with the power to affect: 'It is not about "ideas" but about the production of affecting ideas (*idées affect-antes*)'.[10] As we have seen, this link between affect and idea is also at the core of the psychoanalytical process of identification envisaged as a signifying practice that includes both a cognitive and an affective dimension.

Moreover, we also find in Spinoza the thesis that the social link is of a libidinal nature. For him, indicates Lordon:

> The relational form which defines the political body
> concretely derives from the common affect that brings
> the part together – in a certain way. Envisaged from
> the viewpoint of the parts, the political body is thus a
> question of affects. Human individuals do not form
> political groupings through some rational, contractu
> alist process of deliberation: it is affects which hold
> them together, and it is worth repeating that these
> affects are the vehicle for ideas, values and a common
> symbolic realm.[11]

Thanks to insights from discourse analysis, Spinoza, and psychoanalysis, we can begin to understand why it is so important for the left to discard the rationalist approach that prevents apprehending what is at stake in political struggle and the crucial role played by affects and identification. What moves people to act are affects, and while ideas are indeed important, their power depends on being connected to affects. The pursuit of an ideal of rationality free from affects, which is the aim of so much of democratic political theory, besides being a self-defeating theoretical enterprise, has disastrous consequences when it is taken as a guide for political practice.

To illustrate my argument about the importance of mobilizing affects, let's take the example of the case of the 2019 elections in the United Kingdom. It was a confrontation between the Conservative Party led by Boris Johnson and the Labour Party under the leadership of Jeremy Corbyn. On the side of the Tories there was almost no programme except for a couple of slogans – 'Take Back Control' and 'Get Brexit Done' – that gave people a feeling of empowerment. Labour, after a promising left populist start to the campaign, ended up, because of internal fights, presenting an elaborate programme with a long list of good policies, but it did not seek to awaken affects. The programme was along the lines of 'vote for us and we will give you that, and that, and that', all progressive policies but offered in a 'clientelist' way. The result was, of course, a resounding victory for the Tories.

I am aware that things were particularly difficult for Labour because Brexit played a crucial role in that election. Brexit provided the Tories with a hegemonic signifier that generated strong affects which were able to mobilize a wide range of people. Nevertheless, I think that some lessons can be learned by contrasting the two strategies. Especially when we compare the strategies followed by Labour in the 2017 and 2019 elections.

In the 2017 election, Labour had a powerful left populist rallying cry, 'For the Many, Not the Few', that aimed to establish a political frontier. This enabled them to mobilize political passions, and it resulted in an unexpectedly good result. Unfortunately, this strategy was abandoned in the following election in favour of a more traditional one. The point I want to make is not, of course, that Labour in 2019 should have been imitating the Tories by mobilizing around empty slogans, but that it is not enough to have a good programme. To succeed, the party needs to meet affects and empower people instead of treating them as passive recipients of policies designed by experts who know best.

It is certainly not easy for left forces to face the challenge represented by the rise of right-wing movements because they cannot resort to the demagogic techniques used by their opponents. But I contend that their refusal to acknowledge the central place of passions in politics, and their insistence on only relying on rational arguments, is at the core of their incapacity to design a successful response to the right-wing populist offensive.

4
A Green Democratic Revolution

In chapter 1, I signalled that the pandemic emerged in the context of an ecological emergency caused by global warming. It is now time to examine the nature of this emergency. Although it is only in the past fifty years that the awareness of global warming and its possible consequences for the survival of our societies has become a decisive political issue, movements to protect the living environment have existed for a long time in different forms. As André Gorz noted in *Ecologica*: 'The ecological movement was born long before the deterioration of the environment and the quality of life posed a question of survival for humanity. It was originally born of a spontaneous protest against the destruction of everyday culture by the economic and administrative power apparatus.'[1]

A turning point was reached fifty years ago. In 1972, the Club of Rome published the report *The Limits to Growth*, drawing global attention to the fact that economic growth could not continue indefinitely because of resource depletion. This was also the year in which the first Earth Summit in Stockholm brought together world leaders under the aegis of the United Nations to lay the foundation for global environmental governance. Various international gatherings stimulated research on the environment and the origin of ecological problems, a field that played an increasingly important role in the following years. Thanks to the subsequent emergence of ecologically focused 'green' political parties and the rise of various ecological forms of militancy, the critique of an economic model based on limitless growth began to be recognized as a legitimate political concern. Yet at first ecological demands did not acquire a central role; they were seen as one demand among many others that a progressive politics had to consider.

Today, the situation is different. The multiplication of weather-related natural disasters has helped raise awareness of the urgent need to stabilize the climate. Moreover, it is now generally admitted that human activity is responsible for the ecological crisis. Many scientific studies have proved that global warming is the consequence of the accumulation of greenhouse gas emissions caused by the fossil fuel industries and that it is necessary to curtail them. Since 2018, thanks to youth movements such as Greta Thunberg's Fridays for Future, the question of climate change has acquired an unexpected salience among wide sections of the public. A growing part of the population is now aware that the preservation of acceptable living conditions on earth will depend on the ability to effectively combat global warming. The crucial question is no longer if we need to decarbonize our economies, but how, and how quickly.

Despite a large consensus among ecologists of all stripes on the necessity to move to renewable energy, the path to follow is far from agreed upon. Even among progressive parties no consensus exists about the strategy to follow.[2] One of the main disagreements concerns the possibility of effectuating the ecological transition without radical systemic change.

Many ecological parties believe in the possibility of reaching a consensus on the policies that need to be implemented to decarbonize the economy. They are convinced that, since this objective is in the interest of everybody, all reasonable citizens should be able to agree on the measures needed. They warn against attempts to politicize climate issues, claiming that it might create artificial divisions and impede the wide collaboration necessary for the implementation of a sustainable model of society.

In line with this position, most ecological parties avoid taking sides in the confrontation between left and right, and declare themselves to be situated beyond such an axis. This explains why some are ready to enter in coalitions with both right and left political parties, as is the case in Germany and Austria.

From a left populist perspective, the more interesting propositions are those that, like the Green New Deal, advocate a radical ecological bifurcation which involves a rupture with financial capitalism. Such a project is often associated with the arguments used in the United States by the Sunrise Movement and Alexandra Ocasio Cortez, who, on 5 February 2019, presented a path-breaking resolution to deal with climate change to the US Congress. The resolution had the following goals: To reach net-zero greenhouse gas emissions through a fair and just transition for all communities and workers. To create millions of good, high-wage jobs and ensure prosperity and economic security for all people of the United States. To invest in the infrastructure and industry of the United States to sustainably meet the challenges of the twenty-first century. To secure clean air and water, climate and community resilience, healthy food, access to nature, and a sustainable environment for all. To promote justice and equity by stopping current, as well as preventing future and repairing historical, oppression of frontline and vulnerable communities.

The idea of a Green New Deal has actually been discussed since 2008 in various circles in the United Kingdom. A group of economists led by Ann Pettifor was scrutinizing the close links between the financial and economic sectors and the ecosystem. They claimed that in order to address the climate crisis it was necessary to have a radical intervention of the state to regulate the financial system. Furthermore, they stressed the urgency of subordinating the financial sector to the interests of society and the future of the planet. Societies, they asserted, should abandon their dependency on the economic system of globalized financial capitalism that produces ecological disasters as well as economic, political, and social inequalities.[3]

The American version of the Green New Deal is more comprehensive because it explicitly links the reduction of greenhouse gas emissions with the objective of fixing social problems. It proposes concrete policies to bring solutions to three fundamental problems: the climate crisis, issues of poverty, and racial inequalities. In order to secure the support of the popular sectors whose jobs will be affected, it contains several important proposals which establish strong links between social, economic, and environmental policies, and prioritizes equality. One of its central ideas is to guarantee work to every unemployed American who wants to work in the construction of infrastructures that respect criteria of efficient energy.

In Britain, the Green Industrial Revolution spelled out in the Labour Party programme under Jeremy Corbyn in 2019 also asserted that social and economic justice cannot be separated from environmental justice. The election manifesto announced that Labour would create one million jobs in the UK to transform industry, energy, transportation, agriculture, and construction, while restoring the natural environment. It would promote measures for a rapid decarbonization of the economy, jointly with investment in sustainable, well-paid, and unionized jobs. It would also create new industries to revive the parts of the country that had been neglected, while working in partnership with the workforce and trade unions in every sector of the economy.

The manifesto also announced that Labour would bring energy and water under democratic public ownership and that they would be treated as rights rather than commodities. Any surplus was to be reinvested or used to reduce bills. Emphasis was put on the fact that public ownership secured democratic control over nationally strategic infrastructures and provided collective stewardship for key natural resources. These measures should bring about a radical decentralization of power in order to give local people and communities greater control over their lives and prospects.

All these different proposals call for an ecological bifurcation that articulates demands of both an ecological and social nature. Their objective is to put the ecological struggle in relation with other types of struggles to create a just and more democratic society. By establishing a political frontier and defining an adversary, they contribute to politicizing ecological issues.

The climate movement must be politicized in order to take into consideration the centrality of labour exploitation, while at the same time social struggles must recognize the urgency of global warming. As defenders of the US Green New Deal assert in *A Planet to Win*:

> A Left populism that mobilizes a genuinely multiracial working class is an essential step in the path to creating a more equal and just society – one that can weather climate change and prevent its most catastrophic effects. That kind of politics draws a sharp line between the masses of the excluded and exploited who are likely to suffer the most, and the rich and powerful who benefit from the status quo.[4]

Although under different labels, other projects also aim at a radical ecological bifurcation. For example, *L'avenir en commun* of Jean-Luc Mélenchon's party La France Insoumise. In their programme for l'Union Populaire in the 2022 presidential elections examining the major challenges today, the party advocates a radical change of course and proposes a series of measures to implement an ambitious state-led ecological strategy. This includes 200 billion euros in investments for ecological and social programmes and a vast plan to adapt infrastructures to climate change. Key measures consist in enshrining the principle of the 'green rule' in the constitution, whereby no more is taken from nature than can be replenished and collectivizing fundamental common goods such as water and air by democratically controlling their use and protection. Other proposals include establishing an ecological and solidarity-based protectionism to produce in France and a re-localized, diversified, and ecological agriculture that would create 300,000 jobs, fighting against precarious contracts, re-establishing a protective unemployment insurance, rolling back privatization, and introducing a tax for financial transactions. *L'avenir en commun* stresses the democratic character of this ecological bifurcation and declares: 'We must reorganise the republican state according to ecological and democratic objectives. Ecological planning must be based on the commune, the vital level of democracy.'[5]

At the difference of proposals, like the Green Deal of the European Union, these projects recognize that a real ecological transition cannot take place without a confrontation with financial capitalism. It demands breaking with the dominant regime of accumulation characterized by unprecedented financialization and the globalization of capital indexed to the growth of polluting industries. Although disagreements exist about the forms it should take, the struggle to end the fossil fuel industry is generally considered to be of uppermost importance. This industry is responsible for most of the greenhouse gas emissions that cause global warming and ocean acidification. Moreover, it leads to serious environmental damage to local communities.

While the fight against fossil fuels is a priority for stopping global warming, it will not be enough to achieve an ecological bifurcation capable of delivering a new model of development that guarantees democratic rights and social justice. As indicated by the Chinese government's recent announcement of a plan to reach carbon neutrality by 2060 at the latest, such an objective is perfectly compatible with an authoritarian model. And various forms of 'green capitalism' might also be able to find ways to thrive without exploiting fossil fuels.

Those who promote a Green New Deal are aware of the magnitude of the problem:

> For a stable climate and more equal world, we have to simultaneously unmake our fossil-fuelled lifestyles and build infrastructures that equitably distribute renewable energy. We have to dismantle the most powerful industry on earth incredibly fast, or the things that we build to replace it won't matter. This means tackling fossil capital head on.[6]

They also state, 'A radical Green New Deal leans in to the inevitable intersections of social, economic, and environmental policy, and prioritized equality.'[7]

While these proposals are vital, a project that aims to address the ecological question in its multiple dimensions cannot be limited to the struggle against capitalism, as if a bifurcation only needed to take place at the level of production. As historian Dipesh Chakrabarty argues:

> While there is no denying that climate change has profoundly to do with the history of capital, a critique that is only a critique of capital is not sufficient for addressing questions relating to human history once the crisis of climate change has been acknowledged and the Anthropocene has begun to loom on the horizon of our present.[8]

The Anthropocene is a term coined in the 1980s and later popularized by the atmospheric chemist Paul J. Crutzen. In 2000, Crutzen used the term to signal the beginning of a new geological age in which humans have become the dominant force shaping the earth's climate. However, there are disagreements concerning the term's beginnings and main features. Some people prefer to speak of the 'Capitalocene' to indicate the epoch's links with the development of capitalism, or the 'Plantationcene' to take account of the central significance of slavery and the plantation system in the Americas in producing the current environmental crisis. This debate has given rise to extensive and diverse literature.[9] Nonetheless, I will limit myself here to the insights in the works associated with the Anthropocene that I find important in the political domain.

Far-reaching consequences can be drawn from the recognition that we have entered a new phase of planetary history with a new climatic regime that endangers the very existence of life on earth. The Anthropocene raises a whole series of philosophical and anthropological issues about the relationship between nature and culture, humans and non-humans. To accept that we are part of nature forces us to adopt a different attitude towards the non-human and to challenge some of the basic tenets of modernity.[10]

It could indeed be pointed out that the rationalism defended by the philosophers of the Enlightenment, whose effects in the political field I discussed in chapter 2, is also responsible for the project of domination of Nature that has led to the Anthropocene. Their rationalist ambition to visualize progress as free from both affects and nature is at the origin of the modern project that sees nature as an infinite resource that could, thanks to infinite technical development, be used to carry out infinite growth.

There are those who claim that the critique of this ambition should make us reject the whole modern project. However, I believe that, just as we are able to break the link between the democratic project of the Enlightenment and its foundation in a rationalist epistemology, we should be able to rescue democratic ideals from the Promethean ambition to dominate nature and the capitalist and colonial socio-economic conditions that allowed the pursuit of this ambition. This requires conceiving democracy differently, questioning the privileged place attributed to a certain conception of freedom as emancipation from all forms of constraints, natural and social, and reclaiming the central value of equality that was eclipsed by the hegemony of liberal discourse. The democratic project must be redefined, freeing it from rationalistic biases, and it should make room for the recognition of the needs of non-humans.

In 1985, reflecting on the emergence of new forms of conflict in *Hegemony and Socialist Strategy*, Ernesto Laclau and I argued in favour of connecting the demands of the working class with those of the 'social movements'.[11] Furthermore, we proposed envisaging socialism as the 'radicalization of democracy' – the extension of democratic ideals to a wide range of social relations.

With the ecological crisis, the project of radicalizing democracy has acquired a new dimension. During the twentieth century, the core of the socialist project was the question of inequality and the fight for social justice, conceived in terms of an equal distribution of the fruits of growth. The struggles of the new social movements add new perspectives to the question of social justice but their focus is on autonomy and liberty, and apart from some ecological movements, they do not fundamentally target the nature of growth.

With the new climatic regime, we have entered a phase in which the struggle for social justice requires questioning the productivist and extractivist models. Growth has ceased being considered a source of protection and has become a danger for the material conditions of social reproduction. It is no longer possible to envisage radicalizing democracy without including the end of the model of growth that endangers the existence of society and whose destructive effects are particularly felt by the more vulnerable groups.

Addressing the new climatic regime requires articulating the anti-neoliberal struggle with the ecological one.

The democratic project needs to be reformulated in view of the ecological exigency, and this involves struggles both at the level of production and at the level of reproduction – that is, reproduction understood in the wide sense of the totality of life on the planet, not only human reproduction. Therefore, a critique focused exclusively on capitalism is insufficient and needs to be complemented by concerns about the Anthropocene.

There is another issue I need to raise. While I find proposals for a Green New Deal essential to envisage the policies necessary to fight neoliberalism and its deleterious consequences for the climate, I do not think that those proposals have the capacity, on their own, to generate the common affects that the collective will for carrying out an ecological bifurcation requires. As we have seen, for ideas to acquire force, it is necessary that they meet affects. To awaken affects, ideas need to connect with what Cornelius Castoriadis refers to as the 'imaginary significations' that institute the social world proper to a society.[12]

In many societies, it is the affective force of the democratic imaginary that has provided the significations that motivate people to act. As recent popular mobilizations testify, democratic values, despite their relegation by neoliberalism, still play an important role in the democratic social and political imaginary. This imaginary is constituted by a repertoire of social significations that are transformed through the effects of a plurality of discursive practices. One of its nodal points is the signifier 'democracy', but it is a floating signifier whose meaning is only partially fixed and varies according to different types of articulation. In the nineteenth century, under the impact of socialism, the democratic imaginary was profoundly transformed by the incorporation of social demands. And with the new climatic regime, we are now witnessing new forms of articulation of the democratic ideal. For instance, several proposals have been made to re-signify the meaning of 'rights', and diverse initiatives to attribute rights to non-human entities like rivers or forests have taken places in different countries. In 2017, three countries assigned rights and legal statutes to rivers: the Atrato in Colombia, the Whanganui in New Zealand and the Ganges, and the Yamuna in India.[13]

To be able to bring about the necessary ecological bifurcation, the articulation of anti-neoliberal and ecological struggles needs to mobilize affects of political and ecological nature whose articulation can result in the construction of a 'people'. As I have repeatedly clarified, a 'people' is not a sociological category but a discursive construction with a symbolic and libidinal dimension. It consists in federating a diversity of democratic demands and its construction necessitates a principle of articulation, a 'hegemonic signifier' around which common affects can crystallize. Thanks to this hegemonic signifier, a chain of equivalence can be established among heterogeneous demands to make them coalesce in a 'we' that will act towards a common aim, despite the differences among its components.

What is the hegemonic signifier that could activate the political and ecological affects for creating such a people? I propose envisaging the ecological bifurcation advocated by the Green New Deal in terms of a 'Green Democratic Revolution' as a new front in the radicalization of democracy that redefines democratic principles and then extends them to new fields and a plurality of social relations. Understood in that way, the Green Democratic Revolution reactivates and enriches the democratic imaginary and procures the hegemonic signifier needed to create a chain of equivalence. It would play the role of a 'myth' in the sense of Georges Sorel, an idea whose power to anticipate the future gives a new figure to the present. It is a narrative that conveys affects that could be more powerful and more credible than competing neoliberal discourses and provide the impulse for the creation of a social majority.

The survival of the planet and the conditions that make it habitable is an objective that concerns a great number of people as well as various movements with heterogeneous demands. Besides trade unions and groups organized around socio-economic issues, we find people involved in a variety of feminist, anti-racist, anti-colonial, and LGBTQ+ struggles. In ordinary circumstances, they generally insist on pursuing their own interests, but in view of the seriousness of the ecological crisis, they might become aware of the need to unite to face the forces responsible for the climate emergency and prevent the advent of authoritarian solutions. All their demands are democratic demands, albeit in different ways, and given their shared opposition to autocracy, they can identify with the vision offered by the Green Democratic Revolution. It is a project that could generate powerful affects across a diversity of groups and resonate with the demands of those who are calling for security and protection while also fighting for equality and against different forms of oppression.

For such an identification to take place it is not necessary that the participants share the same world view, and they can have different religious or philosophical convictions. Their concern for the environment can proceed from different sources and they can follow a diversity of approaches, but these differences should not constitute an insurmountable obstacle. Those involved do not have to agree on a fully fledged political programme. Some will define their aims in terms of 'eco-socialism', others will prefer thinking in terms of a 'citizen revolution'.[14] What they share is a common adversary and the will to maintain a habitable planet to secure the future of a democratic society that can give them the opportunity to pursue their specific struggles in a multiplicity of agonistic public spaces.

By advocating a Green Democratic Revolution, I have been delineating how I think the left populist strategy should currently be envisaged. I contend that such a strategy is the most appropriate for articulating the manifold democratic struggles against different forms of domination, exploitation, and discrimination with the defence of the habitability of the planet. The strength of a left populist strategy lies in acknowledging the partisan character of politics and the importance of mobilizing common affects in the construction of a 'we' by drawing a political frontier.

The Green Democratic Revolution asserts that, to bring about a real ecological bifurcation, it is imperative to confront the powerful economic forces that resist it and to break with the neoliberal order. But it also accentuates the democratic character of this bifurcation and visualizes this rupture according to the strategy Erik Olin Wright defines as 'eroding capitalism'.[15] The objective is not to 'smash' capitalism but to displace it through the implementation of a series of what André Gorz calls 'non-reformist' reforms and the development of alternative institutions such as cooperative and bottom-up civil-society-centred initiatives that promote economic activities embodying egalitarian relations.

The state needs to be a significant actor in a Green Democratic Revolution because, as many economists recognize, it will not be possible to achieve the necessary transition to renewable energies without ecological planning. It is illusory to imagine that the profound transformations the ecological bifurcation requires could be made by social movements alone. Activists and ecological groupings have an important role to play, but without winning elections and reaching state power it will not be possible to create the conditions to successfully confront the power of fossil capital. To be able to exercise influence on the decisions taken at state level, it is necessary to organize politically. All those who are involved in diverse ecological struggles should realize that they will not be able to make decisive advances if they shun electoral politics.

Envisaging the necessary ecological bifurcation as a Green Democratic Revolution could, I believe, provide the strategy that the left needs to successfully thwart the attempts to harness the sense of vulnerability produced by the social, economic, and climatic crises, and the affects it has generated, to promote authoritarian forms of security and protection. These demands can be articulated in a progressive way, and it would be a serious mistake to neglect them. At the moment, when neoliberalism is trying to recuperate these demands for authoritarian purposes, it is imperative for the left to impede such a move by articulating the idea of protection with the defence of the habitability of the planet, conceiving it in line with what Paolo Gerbaudo calls 'protectivism', which he defines as follows: 'Protectivism encompasses a great variety of policies, including social welfare, workers' representation, environmental protection and other social support mechanisms.'[16] A Green Democratic Revolution aims to defend society and its material conditions of existence and provide security and protection in a way that empowers people instead of making them retreat into defensive nationalism or a passive acceptance of algorithmic forms of governmentality.

Such a project could federate a wide variety of democratic demands because it addresses the challenge of the new climatic regime while providing social justice and fostering solidarity. Activating passions that are central to the democratic imaginary should motivate people to get involved in politics with the aim of establishing the conditions for a society where the democratic principles of liberty and equality are redefined and extended to new domains, including humans and non-humans. I contend that, understood in this way, the left populist strategy is more relevant than ever.

Postscript

This book had just been completed as the war in Ukraine broke out. It is difficult at this point to assess its possible repercussions. Although territorially localized, the Russian invasion has global consequences and is already having a profound impact in many areas. We suddenly find ourselves in a different conjuncture, forced to face new challenges. In addition to those linked to the economic and social crisis caused by the pandemic and to the ecological emergency, which were the object of my analysis, there are now geopolitical ones whose effects will probably be far-reaching.

We can already see how the war has overshadowed the publication of the latest IPCC report on climate change, and there is real danger of significant regression in the fight against global warming. As of now, many governments are reconsidering their energy policies, and several are already questioning the commitments they have made to reduce greenhouse gases. Taking advantage of the situation, the fossil fuel industries are busy launching an offensive to block the measures aimed at controlling their expansion. Efforts to move away from dependence on Russian fossil fuels might lead to over-investment in the infrastructure needed for liquefied natural gas, which has a larger carbon footprint than gas transported through pipelines. Moreover, we should expect a considerable increase in military spending at the expense of the investments necessary for the energy transition.

This is a decisive moment in the fight for a radicalization of democracy. A new dimension is being added to the demands for security and protection that, as I have pointed out, are currently being exploited by the neoliberal forces to buy time. Indeed, the awareness of the dangers of energy dependency could play in their favour and reinforce their power. But the need to break the dependence on Russian gas could also be seen as a sign of the importance of accelerating the move towards renewable energies. The left must seize this chance. Intense moments of crisis provide an occasion to choose between clearly defined alternatives. The future will depend on the way people perceive the situation and on the possibility of convincing them of the necessity of quickening the process of ecological bifurcation. This should be done by deploying a left populist strategy articulating social struggles with ecological struggles around the project of a Green Democratic Revolution.

The war in Ukraine, and the wide range of reactions it has generated, constitutes a clear refutation of the inadequacy of the rationalist approach to politics. To be sure, it brings to the fore the dangerous role that affects can play, but it also reveals how they can contribute to the construction of a more democratic society. This is why understanding the part played by affects and the importance of mobilizing them in a progressive direction is so crucial in politics.

Acknowledgements

I am grateful to Leticia Sabsay, Yannis Stavrakakis, and Erna von der Walde for helpful suggestions on several aspects of the book.

I would also like to thank my editor at Verso, Leo Hollis, for his support.

Notes

1. A New Authoritarian Form of Neoliberalism

1. Chantal Mouffe, *For a Left Populism* (London: Verso, 2018); Ernesto Laclau and Chantal Mouffe, *Hegemony and Socialist Strategy: Towards a Radical Democratic Politics* (London: Verso, 1985); Ernesto Laclau, *On Populist Reason* (London: Verso, 2005).
2. Chantal Mouffe, *On the Political* (Abingdon: Routledge, 2005).
3. Andrew Gamble, *The Free Economy and the Strong State: The Politics of Thatcherism* (Durham, NC: Duke University Press, 1988).
4. David Harvey, *A Brief History of Neoliberalism* (Oxford: Oxford University Press, 2005), p. 2.
5. Luc Boltanski and Eve Chiapello, *The New Spirit of Capitalism* (London and New York: Verso, 2005).
6. Chantal Mouffe, *Agonistics: Thinking the World Politically* (London and New York: Verso, 2013), Chapter 4.
7. Wolfgang Streeck, *Buying Time: The Delayed Crisis of Democratic Capitalism* (London and New York: Verso, 2014).

8. Ibid., p. 17.
9. Karl Polanyi, *The Great Transformation* (Boston: Beacon Press, 1991).
10. Naomi Klein, 'The Screen New Deal', *The Intercept*, 8 May 2020.
11. Evgeny Morozov, *To Save Everything, Click Here: The Folly of Technological Solutionism* (New York: Public Affairs, 2013).

2. Politics and Affects

1. Ernesto Laclau and Chantal Mouffe, *Hegemony and Socialist Strategy: Towards a Radical Democratic Politics* (London : Verso, 1985).
2. Oliver Marchart, *Post-foundational Political Thought* (Edinburgh: Edinburgh University Press, 2007).
3. Ludwig Wittgenstein, *Culture and Value* (Chicago: University of Chicago Press, 1984), p. 64.
4. Chantal Mouffe, *The Democratic Paradox* (London: Verso, 2000).
5. Pierre Saint-Amand, *The Laws of Hostility: Politics, Violence and the Enlightenment* (Minneapolis: University of Minnesota Press, 1996).
6. Albert Hirschman, *The Passions and the Interests: Political Arguments for Capitalism before Its Triumph* (Princeton, NJ: Princeton University Press, 1977).
7. Jürgen Habermas, *The Philosophical Discourse of Modernity* (Cambridge, MA: MIT Press, 1987).
8. Hans Blumenberg, *The Legitimacy of the Modern Age* (Cambridge, MA: MIT Press, 1983).
9. Ibid., p. 65, emphasis in original.
10. Richard Rorty, 'Against Belatedness', *London Review of Books* 5:11, 1983.

11. Chantal Mouffe, *Agonistics: Thinking the World Politically* (London: Verso, 2013).

12. Chantal Mouffe, *On the Political* (London and New York: Routledge, 2005).

3. Affects, Identity, and Identification

1. Sigmund Freud, *Group Psychology and the Analysis of the Ego*, in *The Standard Edition of the Complete Psychological Works of Sigmund Freud*, vol. 18 (London: Vintage, 2001), p. 92.

2. Yannis Stavrakakis, 'Passions of Identification: Discourse, Enjoyment, and European Identity', in *Discourse Theory in European Politics*, ed. David Howarth and Jacob Torfing (Basingstoke: Palgrave Macmillan, 2005), p. 69.

3. Ibid., p. 72, emphasis in original.

4. Yannis Stavrakakis, *Lacan and the Political* (London and New York: Routledge, 1999), p. 30.

5. Stavrakakis, 'Passions of Identification', p. 72, emphasis in original.

6. Yannis Stavrakakis, *The Lacanian Left* (Edinburgh: Edinburgh University Press, 2007), p. 190.

7. Ibid., p. 200.

8. Ibid., p. 215.

9. Ernst Bloch, *Heritage of Our Times* (Cambridge: Polity, 1991).

10. Frédéric Lordon, *Les affects de la politique* (Paris: Editions du Seuil, 2016), p. 57.

11. Frédéric Lordon, *Imperium: Structures and Affects of Political Bodies* (London: Verso, 2022), p. 116.

4. A Green Democratic Revolution

1. André Gorz, *Ecologica* (Paris: Galilée, 2008), p. 48.
2. For a thoughtful discussion of the different approaches, see Amanda Machin, *Negotiating Climate Change: Radical Democracy and the Illusion of Consensus* (London and New York: Zed Books, 2013).
3. Ann Pettifor, *The Case for the Green New Deal* (London: Verso, 2019).
4. Kate Aronoff, Alyssa Battistoni, Daniel Aldana Cohen, and Thea Riofrancos, *A Planet to Win: Why We Need a Green New Deal* (London: Verso, 2019), p. 183.
5. Jean-Luc Mélenchon, *L'avenir en commun* (Paris: Editions du Seuil, 2021), p. 45, author's translation.
6. Ibid., p. 31.
7. Ibid., p. 19.
8. Dipesh Chakrabarty, 'The Climate of History: Four Theses', *Critical Inquiry* 35:2, Winter 2009, p. 212.
9. A good presentation of the literature can be found in Christophe Bonneuil and Jean-Baptiste Fressoz, *The Shock of the Anthropocene: The Earth, History and Us* (London and New York: Verso, 2016).
10. The best discussion of this challenge is found in Pierre Charbonnier, *Affluence and Freedom: An Environmental History of Political Ideas* (Cambridge: Polity, 2021).
11. Ernesto Laclau and Chantal Mouffe, *Hegemony and Socialist Strategy: Towards a Radical Democratic Politics* (London: Verso, 1985).
12. Cornelius Castoriadis, *World in Fragments: Writing on Politics, Society, Psychoanalysis, and Imagination* (Stanford: Stanford University Press, 1997), pp. 10–13.
13. María Ximena González Serrano, 'Blog Series "Nature and Its Rights": Young Researcher's Seminar April 2020', river-ercproject.eu.

14. For an eloquent defence of the eco-socialist vision, see Paul Magnette, *La vie large* (Paris: La Découverte, 2022).
15. Erik Olin Wright, *How to Be an Anti-capitalist in the Twenty-First Century* (London and New York: Verso, 2019).
16. Paolo Gerbaudo, *The Great Recoil: Politics after Populism and Pandemic* (London: Verso, 2021), p. 112.

Index